YOU WILL GET THROUGH THIS

Faith, Hope & Help for Your Trying Times

LUCIA DEY

YOU WILL GET THROUGH THIS

Faith, Hope & Help for Your Trying Times

LUCIA DEY

You Will Get Through This
Trilogy Christian Publishers A Wholly Owned Subsidiary of Trinity Broadcasting Network
2442 Michelle Drive Tustin, CA 92780
Copyright © 2021 by Lucia Dey

Scripture quotations marked NIV are taken from the Holy Bible, New International Version®, NIV®. Copyright © 1973, 1978, 1984, 2011 by Biblica, Inc.™ Used by permission of Zondervan. All rights reserved worldwide. www.zondervan.com. The "NIV" and "New International Version" are trademarks registered in the United States Patent and Trademark Office by Biblica, Inc.™ Scripture quotations marked NKJV are taken from the New King James Version®. Copyright © 1982 by Thomas Nelson. Used by permission. All rights reserved. Scripture quotations marked nlt are taken from the Holy Bible, New Living Translation, copyright © 1996, 2004, 2015 by Tyndale House Foundation. Used by permission of Tyndale House Publishers, Inc., Carol Stream, Illinois 60188. All rights reserved. Scripture quotations marked kjv are taken from the King James Version of the Bible. Public domain.

No part of this book may be reproduced, stored in a retrieval system, or transmitted by any means without written permission from the author. All rights reserved. Printed in the USA.
Rights Department, 2442 Michelle Drive, Tustin, CA 92780.
Trilogy Christian Publishing/TBN and colophon are trademarks of Trinity Broadcasting Network. For information about special discounts for bulk purchases, please contact Trilogy Christian Publishing.
Trilogy Disclaimer: The views and content expressed in this book are those of the author and may not necessarily reflect the views and doctrine of Trilogy Christian Publishing or the Trinity Broadcasting Network.
Manufactured in the United States of America
10 9 8 7 6 5 4 3 2 1
Library of Congress Cataloging-in-Publication Data is available.
B-ISBN#: 978-1-63769-832-7
E-ISBN#: 978-1-63769-833-4

Correspond with the author via:
Email: info@luciadey.org
Website: www.luciadey.org

ACKNOWLEDGMENTS

I want to thank God first because without God, I would not have been able to do anything. He gave me life and wisdom, and everything I have is from Him.

To my parents, Mr. and Mrs. Ambrose Kojo Dey, especially my sweet mother, Rebecca Aku Appekey Dey, thank you for always being the person I could turn to during those dark and desperate times. She sustained me in several ways. Besides giving birth to me, my mom rescued me on some occasions by donating blood to save my life due to my sickle cell disease. In some instances, my mom had to sell her clothes and cows in order to pay for my hefty hospital bills to keep me going. Even at times when I thought of giving up in life, she would say in Dangbe, *"Mawu be dzi be,"* meaning *"God's timing is the best. Never give up, my beautiful little girl."*

To my little brother, Apostle Nicholas, and my big brothers—Raymond and James Dey: Thank you for letting me know that you had nothing but great memories of me despite having no contact for about eighteen years. Even on those days that I felt alone, your continuous encouraging communication and video chats kept me going, and I cherish those very much.

Also, to all my twenty-four siblings (half-brothers and sisters), I am so thankful to have you all in my life. *I love my Dey clan!*

Writing a book is harder than I thought and more rewarding than I ever imagined. None of this would have been possible without good friends like Christopher Y. Fodo. He was the first friend I made when I migrated to the United States of America. He picked me up from the airport on the day I landed in America. He taught me how to drive. He stood by me during every struggle and all my successes. That is true friendship. *Thanks, and God bless you, Uncle Chris.*

I am eternally grateful to my best friend, brother and mentor. Minister Samuel Ansah, who took in an extra mouth to feed when he didn't have to. He taught me discipline, love, manners, respect, and so much more that has helped me succeed in life. I truly have no idea where I would be if he did not take a chance on a twenty-three-year-old girl and let her fly to him in Virginia, America, or become the father figure whom she desperately needed since high school in Ghana. He never considered my age or gender. He is a total stranger God sent my way, who just saw me as a young girl, hungry to learn, hungry to grow, yearning for a change, and hungry to succeed in life. He never stopped me; he only encouraged me. God bless you, Minister Sam (my hero), your lovely wife Aunty Diana, and your beautiful children Samuel Junior, Angela, and Christopher. *Blessings to my*

ACKNOWLEDGMENTS

Ansah family always!

Also, special thanks to my dearest sister Rebecca Ayettey, aka Aunty Naa Baa. You epitomize strong sisterhood and could take over the world if you wanted. Your endless spiritual and business partnership, editorial help, keen insight, and ongoing support in bringing my stories to life earned you the "First Best Girlfriend" title in the book of my life. Much love always, boss!

An incredible special shout-out to my little sister from another mother—Lebene Ahiabor, who became a very reliable Personal Assistant to me and my mom. I call her my personal Foreign Affairs Minister because she serves me with all the resources and support I need back home in Ghana. She was kind enough to connect me with Pastor Martin Bedi-Tsatsu, who edited the entire book for literally no charge. Thank you for introducing me to my editor in chief, Pastor Fred.

Writing a book about the story of your life is a surreal process. I am forever indebted to you, Pastor Fred, for your editorial help and support in bringing my stories to life. It is because of your efforts and encouragement that I have a legacy to pass on to my family.

To everyone at BeServed Concierge LLC who enabled me to be the CEO of a company I built from scratch with $250 in the bank, zero loan, and no credit card, I say thank you for letting me serve you, for being a part of your amazing lives, and for showing up every day and helping more seniors enjoy their lives independently in the comfort of their homes. You are true difference makers! Five years and counting…God bless you!

Heartfelt gratitude to all those great men and women of God who have been a part of my getting here:

Rev. Dr. Mensa Otabil (Founder and General Overseer of International Central Gospel Church [ICGC] Worldwide); Pastor Sadick Arthur, his family, and the original Vessels of Worship (VOW) team, and members of ICGC Fulfillment Temple, Springfield, Virginia; Pastor Kojo Amo-Asare; Pastor Rosabella Mensah; Deacon George Ennin (my godfather); Pastor Dr. John Forson; Pastor Kofi Arthur and other known Pastors of ICGC Worldwide; Pastor Samuel Asare and his family of Lord of the Harvest Church, Woodbridge, Virginia; Pastor Daniel Owusu and his family of Throne Room of Grace Church, Manassas, Virginia; the Agamah family in Richmond, VA, especially Vera aka Ms. Pinky; the Anumah family in VA; Mrs. Regina Allotey; Mrs. Endora Boadu (my super cool makeup artist) of Hadassah Artistry; Minister Stine Owusu (my music producer); Minister Helen Light aka Madam Light (the fire girl who inspired and pushed me to get my music mojo back, you are my inspiration for real and I love you!); and Mrs. Grace Enim Yeboah, a unique God-fearing woman whom I have the pleasure of working with at Standard Chartered Bank, High Street/US Embassy, Accra, Ghana. Talking about workplace

ACKNOWLEDGMENTS

evangelism, I learned it from Sister Grace. She influenced my life greatly with the Word of God.

Finally, a big thank you to everyone on my publishing team at Buabeng Books, especially Fred Asante. You made my dream come true in the most challenging time of my life.

For that, I am incredibly grateful!

To you, all my wonderful readers: May God keep you, bless you, and give you peace.

DEDICATION

I dedicate this book to my precious daughter, "Princess" Sasha Samuella Selassie Naa Adjeley, also known as Dr. Ms. Sasha, who has been my inspiration, chief encourager, and cheerleader since day one of this book project. Thank you, CeCe, for making me happy and cheering me on day and night. You are the best gift ever! We thank God every day for blessing us with you.

Also, to you, love, my personal person, Mr. Stephen Sackey. *A big thank you* for being there, loving me in good and bad times. I strongly believe our best days are ahead of us. I will always count you as one of my many blessings! I love you and CeCe very much!

To my heavenly angels: Nicole Atsufe Dey, my younger sister, and Sedem, my first daughter and Prince Selinam, my son, you are always in my heart. Till we meet again in heaven, I love you all very much.

> Matthew 18:10: *"See that you do not despise one of these little ones. For I tell you that their angels in heaven always see the face of my Father in heaven"* (NIV).
>
> Philippians 4:19-20: *"And my God will meet*

YOU WILL GET THROUGH THIS

all your needs according to the riches of his glory in Christ Jesus. To our God and Father be glory for ever and ever. Amen" (NIV).

A TRIBUTE TO A VIRTUOUS WOMAN

A courageous strong woman,
dependent solely on God

"Speak up for those who cannot speak for themselves,
for the rights of all who are destitute.
Speak up and judge fairly; defend
the rights of the poor and needy.

The Wife of Noble Character

A wife of noble character who can find?
She is worth far more than rubies.
Her husband has full confidence in her
and lacks nothing of value.

She brings him good,
not harm, all the days of her life."

Proverbs 31:8-12 (NIV)

Proverbs 31:25: *"She is clothed with strength and dignity; she can laugh at the days to come."*

YOU WILL GET THROUGH THIS

Proverbs 31:26: *"She opens her mouth with wisdom, and the teaching of kindness is on her tongue."*

Proverbs 31:28-29: *"Her children rise up and call her blessed; her husband also, and he praises her: 'Many women have done excellently, but you surpass them all.'"*

Mrs. Rebecca Aku Vena Appekey Dey

I am so gracious for everything you have always been. You are amazing, strong, selfless, and loving, and I'm such a blessed child to have a wonderful mother like you. When I fell and cried, Mom, you were always there to kiss me to make it go away. It is because of you, Mom, that I am stronger. Thank you!

Even when I'm sitting in the dark, you still turn the light on for me. Thank you, Mama. I don't tell you that enough.

I want to thank you for being my mother, for I will never have another. You had every reason to give up on me, especially during the time I was battling sickle cell disease. I used to be so afraid, thinking you might leave me at Bator or Adidome Hospital and never come back, especially watching you physically abused by a German mission doctor on a very hot Sunday at Bator hospital, who thought you intentionally neglected me on purpose. I will never forget that day in my life. Even when some of our own families thought I was a demon-possessed child and tried all means to convince you to give me up, you chose to sacrifice everything so I could become who I am today. Most importantly, you chose Christ over idols so you could pray with me, and you accompanied me to my favorite church activities. You're the best!

As I've grown older, I realize all you give up for me, and I thank you and I hope to do the same for you.

I'm so blessed, mom, that the apples don't fall very far from the tree.

It goes without saying that you are the best mom in the world and I'm so grateful.

You are beautiful and soft around the edges, but you have the strength of steel and I'm eternally grateful that you're mine and I love you, mom.

God bless you always, sweet Mama, aka *Sister!*

TABLE OF CONTENTS

Introduction．．．．．．．．．．．．．．．．．．．．．．．．．．．19

1. The Promises of Hope in Tough Times．．．．．．．．25

2. A Good Purpose for That Bad Story．．．．．．．．．．31

3. Encouraging Others in Our
       Own Discouragement．．．．．．．．．．．．．．．．．．35

4. Building Endurance for the Trials of Life．．．．．．．41

5. How to Hold a Hurting Heart．．．．．．．．．．．．．．45

6. Something Happened in That Small Church．．．．．49

7. Scrubbing Toilets for the Glory of God．．．．．．．．53

8. What Is the "More" God Wants for You?．．．．．．．57

9. Hope in the One Who Does Not Grow Weary．．．．61

10. I Feel Forgotten．．．．．．．．．．．．．．．．．．．．．．．65

11. Difficulties of Living in a Foreign Land．．．．．．．．71

12. Getting Overwhelmed with Living Abroad．．．．．79

13. The Scribbled Truth That Changed My Life．．．．83

14. For Our Own and Heaven's Sake,
    We Tell the Truth. 87

15. Who Do You Listen To? 93

16. Church Is Meant to Be a Grace Trip,
    Not a Guilt Trip 99

17. The End of My "What Ifs" 103

18. An Agenda That Will Never Satisfy 107

19. When We Grow Weary in Waiting 111

Conclusion 123

INTRODUCTION

God understands your struggles: He is merciful and compassionate.

There is no one who can understand us like God. He knows what you are going through and will give a way of escape. Just trust Him.

The thing you just went through may look like a loss, but God is going to take it and work it together for your good!

I am Lucia Dey, and this is my story…

1 Peter 2:9 (NIV)… *"But you are a chosen people, a royal priesthood, a holy nation, God's special possession, that you may declare the praises of him who called you out of darkness into his wonderful light."*

Hey, extraordinary!

Would you believe me if I told you each one of us was put here for a specific purpose? And the unfortunate truth of it is that most of us will never fulfill that purpose. There are many reasons why this is so. Reasons such as fear, uncertainty of the future, a painful past, learned behaviors, and a negative mindset are all common factors that can block us from reaching our highest selves, but at any given moment, we can combat those factors and change the course of our lives. That dream, that feeling in your gut that you can't stop thinking about, is your purpose calling. That vision which is playing like music in your ears is your purpose calling you. I encourage you to feed that dream a little bit each day until it grows like a baby and gets bigger and better. So, *go for it*! Move from thinking in the ordinary to *extraordinary*! Put actions behind your dreams without fear. After all, *fear is not real*. To help make the idea of this easier, let me give you a bit of backstory on myself.

I have always been a dreamer, despite struggling with sickle cell anemia all my life. But after losing my two-year-old daughter and one-week-old son to the same wicked blood disorder, things changed for me. I had allowed my painful past and the opinions of others to dictate the course of my life. I went to Virginia School of Nursing Institute because my friends had that vision for me, even though my gut told me that I wouldn't find my purpose there. Yet, I went anyway because that was what was expected of me. The good thing is God always has a way of showing us a sign to nudge us back on track to our purpose, and the best thing in my situation was, I listened. I was in college with few weeks left to graduate when I chose to rock the title of "college dropout" due to mental illness.

After over a decade of migrating to the United States of America, with no sign of reconnecting with my family after series of filing and interviews, I was seeking answers to

INTRODUCTION

so many questions, including where my two children were buried, why I experienced domestic abuse, why I spent time in jail for no crime, and why God went silent.

So many unanswered questions had made my world very dark. Despite my big faith in God, my continued service, my faithful giving, endless sacrifices in the house of God, regular attendance to prayer services and all kinds of special church events, I felt lost. Sometimes, I felt as if I was living a double life because I smiled and looked beautiful to people outside, but deep down in my heart, I was in pain. A pain I covered so well that nobody could ever see it. After some persistent prayers and talking to some Christian and professional counselors, it became clear that I needed to take time off school and work to take care of myself. This time I *listened*. I took a break for a while. I thought all was well, so I transferred my credits from University College University of Maryland (UMUC) to Northern Virginia Community College (NOVA) and tried to graduate. The closer I got to graduating, the more depressed I became.

I was at the lowest point of my life, and I tried taking my own life on two occasions. I remember it like yesterday; I was so overwhelmed and felt completely out of options, but I decided to pick up my Bible. I can't remember the verse I read, but that night, I went to sleep and had the most vivid dream ever; I knew I was supposed to be a leader. I knew the name of my business and my mission statement. I woke up inspired and wrote them down. Everything revealed to me in that dream was so clear. The only thing that was not revealed was the "how," but deep down, it didn't matter because that one dream brought me *peace* and gave me the urge I needed to step out in faith. I never looked back after that day, and I knew no one and nothing could dictate my future but me. If I wanted to live my life fulfilled, I had to do what felt right.

A fire was lit inside me that night, and it has been burning bright ever since. Now, eight years later, I am a wife, a happy mom, and a full-time entrepreneur with lots of flexibilities. My senior care concierge is helping families across Northern Virginia. Now, I am able to pour into other people financially and spiritually. Most importantly, I get to do God's work every day. It was all part of God's purpose for me, and it was all connected to that dream in my heart. But what if I had not acted? What would have happened? Where would I have been? Would all the seniors and my care partners whom my services helped have found the right solution? I could ask a million questions to drive home the point of how important it is to act on your dreams! Your purpose and the One who gives you life are so much greater than *you*! And when you begin to act without fear and feed your dreams, you can change lives and the world around you. So, dream and *dream big*. Anything you can imagine is real and this world needs you to reach your full potential! I am so grateful to God for giving me so many chances!

INTRODUCTION

How do you keep faith in hard times? My proven 10 steps:

Step 1: Examine Your Heart and Keep a Clean Heart.

Step 2: Meditate Daily on God's Word.

Step 3: Pray with Faith and Talk to God More Often.

Step 4: Renew Your Mind. Positive Thoughts Only.

Step 5: Build Up Your Faith in God.

Step 6: Offer worship, Praise, and Thankfulness

Step 7: Nurture Your Spirit, Soul, and Body.

Step 8: Also, Read Bible Quotes to Encourage Yourself in Tough Times.

Step 9: Be in a Positive and Loving Environment.

Step 10: Shrink Your Circle to Contain Optimistic People Only.

ONE

THE PROMISES OF HOPE IN TOUGH TIMES

Romans 5:5..."And hope does not put us to shame, because God's love has been poured into our hearts through the Holy Spirit who has been given to us."

There is hope! God specializes in healing the holes in our souls and helping us handle life's issues. Who is better to heal our broken souls than the One who \created us and gave us life? We can always take comfort in knowing that God understands and cares about us very much. The Bible teaches us that we do not have a high priest who is unable to empathize with our weaknesses (Hebrew 4:15). Have you ever felt abandoned by God? If yes, then you are not alone.

Broken Within (Maybe Not Even Realizing It)

Life is hard. It can beat us down to the ground. Because of this, people get broken within. They lose heart and hope. I think we can all attest to this at one point or another in our lives—the emptiness, the desperation, and the guilt of sin, all of which cause a broken spirit. I have met many people who are broken, and you know what? Some don't even realize it. They think that is what life is and nothing more.

It is troubling for one to have no hope for the future but just a picture of the next dreary day to face. The only thing they have is the end of the working week, only to be let down by the chores of the weekend and the reminder that Monday is just a couple of days away. Usually, when people want to escape some of these challenges, they turn to the world. Even Christians can get caught up in this cycle of life. We cannot break free from it without being broken, though.

I can think back to my cycles of being broken. I can recall also the many times I got stuck in my troubles and was thinking, *"Woe is me,"* over and over again, feeling sorry for myself, and not facing what the cause of the trouble was. Yes, I have looked to the world for comfort and left Jesus to the wayside, blaming Jesus for my tribulations. I used Jesus as a punching bag with my thoughts and words. Did it help? Not at all, but I did it, nonetheless.

In my mind, I would wrestle with Jesus about my realities and situations. I forgot His promises in my broken state. I would rather be angry at Him than face my realities and the troubles I got myself into. Why didn't He bail me out of my issues? Why did He not give me the strength to avoid the sins I committed? I was so self-absorbed that I could not see the truth in front of me—my actions and inactions placed me in the situations that got me broken within.

The truth of the matter is that I deserved the pains that caused my suffering. But you know what? Satan capitalized on my pity parties and dragged me further from Christ than I would like to admit. Many times, I did not see this happening, but I only found myself in a deep hole, looking up to the small light above. It was my heart Satan was trying to capture and render cold. Thankfully, he failed at each attempt because I was able to come to my senses and reach out to the light, and with Christ's help, climbed out of the holes of brokenness.

You may be facing a similar situation. You may be in your own hole of despair and hopelessness that caused your brokenness. I do not know your situation but let me tell you…you can make it back to Christ.

Satan wants you to stay broken. He wants your hurt to get worse and worse. He would grab you by the ankles and pull you down the hole of nothingness if he gets the opportunity. This can be avoided by making an effort and having a conscious realization of what you are doing to yourself and what Satan is attempting to do to you.

1 Peter 2:24 says, *"Who his own self bare our sins in his own body on the tree, that we, being dead to sins, should live unto righteousness: by whose stripes ye were healed."*

Christ died for us, so we would be seen as right before God. The verse did not say some sins or that we were partly healed. It said "sins" and "healed." This Scripture is not antagonistic, but straightforward and easy to comprehend. It is a simple statement that resonates with our position in Christ.

Whenever we feel broken, we must remember that Jesus died for us. It is our choice to believe this or not. And with the promise of eternity with Him, if we accept His grace and mercy, we should live our lives in joyfulness and not in brokenness.

In Romans 15:13, the Apostle Paul tells us, *"Now the God of hope fill you with all joy and peace in believing, that ye may abound in hope, through the power of the Holy Ghost."*

"Joy and peace in believing." How simple and awesome that is! No strings attached. No conditions attached. No parentheses saying "except." Because of our belief, we can abound in hope. We can hold on to this concept of hope because Christ has given us many promises.

As we suffer through our troubles and hold tight to Christ, we grow stronger in Him. Our relationship with Christ should not be contingent on a good and happy life but on the promises of being with Him in heaven through belief and hope.

As we get closer to Christ, though we may face troubles, or deal with Satan's seeming hold on our lives, or perhaps his attempts to drag us down, all his efforts will be nil. We will not be broken because our hope is in our hearts.

Isn't that what it is all about? Keeping the love and hope in Christ in our hearts? If we can do this, it is unlikely that we will be broken within even in the worst of times. Yes, we will be tempted by Satan to let go of Christ and turn to the world, but these are the times when we need to keep our trust and hope in Christ and let the Holy Spirit lead us.

The Holy Spirit is our helper, not sometimes, but all the time. We just need to listen. The road to brokenness begins with us not listening to the Holy Spirit in our lives. The Holy Spirit does not lead us to failure. If we listen to Him, we will be sure to avoid such troubles. Trouble enters our lives, and we wander around like lost sheep outside the pen when we do not listen to Him.

Some Christians fall because of the brokenness they experience in their lives. They walk away from Jesus and fall into the world to look for answers like I did. Some, though, let go of Jesus, shut the Holy Spirit out, and walk away.

We all know people who have done this. They faced a hard time, blamed God, and never came back. It is sad to see this happen. It reminds me of the parable of the sower in

Matthew 13:1-9. Some of the seeds sprouted up, and when adversity came, they withered and died. They lost sight of Christ and gave up on the hope and promises of Christ.

Look, I am not calling anyone out on this. I am just speaking from my heart because of what I have been through and what I have seen. If a sinner like me could crawl out of the cave of darkness back to Christ, then others can too. You can too. All it takes is seeking Christ in your life again. There is no secret formula or specific words; just talk to Jesus. He will not turn you away but welcome you back with open arms.

"My brethren, count it all joy when ye fall into divers temptations; Knowing this, that the trying of your faith worketh patience. But let patience have her perfect work, that ye may be perfect and entire, wanting nothing" (James 1:2–4).

TWO

A GOOD PURPOSE FOR THAT BAD STORY

> Genesis 41:52 (NIV)..."*The second son he named Ephraim and said, 'It is because God has made me fruitful in the land of my suffering.'*"

I have had some terrible things happening in my life that I would just love to forget soon. I bet you have, too. But as soon as I start to rip out the pages and shred the memories, God says to my soul, "Hold up. I've got a good purpose for that bad story." Truth is, I used to hate talking about my past…but not any longer!

Joseph learned that lesson too. We find his story in Genesis 37–50. Joseph's jealous brothers sold him into slavery. He was falsely accused of sexual assault and was put in a prison to die.

Then God miraculously rescued him from prison and

made him second in command to the Egyptian Pharaoh. By his thirty-seventh birthday, Joseph had two sons. One he named Manasseh, which means, *"God has made me forget all my trouble and all my father's household"* (Genesis 41:51b, NIV). The second son, he named Ephraim, which means, *"It is because God has made me fruitful in the land of my suffering"* (Genesis 41:52b).

Many years after his sons were born, Joseph learned that his father, Jacob (later named Israel), was ill. So, he took his two sons, Manasseh and Ephraim, and traveled for one last visit to see his father. When they arrived, Jacob said, *"Bring them to me so I may bless them"* (Genesis 48:9b, NIV).

Joseph brought his sons to his father's bedside. He placed Ephraim on his right toward Jacob's left hand and Manasseh, his firstborn, on his left toward Jacob's right hand. But instead of giving the blessing to Joseph's firstborn, Jacob reached out his right hand and put it on Ephraim's head, though he was the younger. Then he crossed his arms and put his left hand on Manasseh's head. Joseph tried to stop his father from giving the blessing to the second-born rather than the firstborn, but his father refused:

> *"...I know, my son, I know. He too will become a people, and he too will become great. Nevertheless, his younger brother will be greater than he, and his descendants will become a group of nations"* (Genesis 48:19b, NIV).

So, he put Ephraim ahead of Manasseh. What a beaᴜ picture! Yes, Joseph had a life of trouble, and he suffer the hands of those who abused, neglected, and betrayed him. But God did not want him to merely *forget* his suffering as the name Manasseh implied. He wanted him to be *fruitful in his suffering* as the name Ephraim implied.

It's the same with you and me. God does not want us to simply *forget* the pain of our past. He wants us to be *fruitful* in the land of our suffering and use it for our good.

Years after I experienced secondary infertility and loss of two children, I read Song of Solomon 2:1. The bride said to the groom, *"I am a rose of Sharon..."* Feeling prompted to look up my name, *Lucia*, in the baby names dictionary online, I learned it originated from Italy, meaning a *graceful light or morning star.* God did not want me to just forget my personal pain of losing my children, but to be a light in other ways…to shine in the "darkness" of my suffering by helping others who may be experiencing loss.

God does not comfort us just to make us comfortable. He comforts us to make us *comfort-able*: *to be* able to comfort others with the comfort we have received. So, do not rip out those painful stories and try to forget them, allow God to heal them and then use them. Someone needs to hear your story (2 Corinthians 1:4, NIV).

> Romans 8:28 (NIV): *"And we know that in all things God works for the good of those who*

love him, who have been called according to his purpose."

Romans 15:4 (NIV): *"For everything that was written in the past was written to teach us, so that through the endurance taught in the Scriptures and the encouragement they provide we might have hope."*

THREE

ENCOURAGING OTHERS IN OUR OWN DISCOURAGEMENT

2 Corinthians 12:9 (KJV) says, *"And he said unto me, My grace is sufficient for thee: for my strength is made perfect in weakness. Most gladly therefore will I rather glory in my infirmities, that the power of Christ may rest upon me."*

It is hard to persevere. I am not saying we should give up, not at all. I am just saying it is hard sometimes to keep fighting. Maybe it is just me and I'm way off the mark by saying this, but I think a lot of folks can relate to what I am saying. Life can throw so many things at us.

The world can booby-trap our paths unceasingly to get us to slide away from Christ. Has Satan thrown enough traps at you to get you to just give up? Yes. I know some of you suffer, and it is hard to get through each day, each hour, to just survive. I have been in this boat sailing towards the edge of the abyss, yet I am here, and I am persevering.

One genetic condition that eats me up so much is sickle cell anemia. It is a horrid condition. If you know anyone who lives with it, you at least, have an idea of how miserable the situation can be sometimes. There are so many variations in the pain and ache that come with this condition, such that explaining how it feels becomes very difficult. By His grace, I no longer live on blood transfusions and regular ion shots. Indeed, God is good all the time!

In the normal sense, suffering from sickle cell anemia is like having flu with a normal temperature, periodic episodes of pain, shortness of breath, body aches, fatigue, stomach pain, vision problems, and feet and joint pains, which make wearing shoes very uncomfortable. But this is just the tip of the iceberg. It goes way beyond that, but this is just the normal feeling most of the time.

There are good days, but they are outnumbered by bad days. My journey with sickle cell anemia has been over forty years…a *lifetime*, and I hate it because of the pain, ache, fatigue, and the lack of sleep that come with it. It gets bad sometimes, but I am not a quitter, so I persevere and endure. God is my strength, and though I pray for relief and healing, I trust the Lord in my condition regardless of whether He answers me or not or gives me a night of rest.

I questioned myself, *"Is this a test?"* I remind myself that life is a test of perseverance in the Lord regardless of whether it is a disease, financial crisis, temptation, or tribulation. We just need to learn to trust in the Lord and persevere. So, when I am talking about it here, I am not talking out of the side of my mouth; I am living it, just like you.

Is perseverance easy? Oh no! If it were, it would not be called perseverance, would it? I have to look at each day as a day the Lord has made, to be glad and rejoice in it. Now you see why I like to smile. Easy? Hardly, especially when facing something, would you see it in the rear-view mirror of life. Before I go to bed for those few hours of slumber, I am always hoping and praying for a better day and the strength to face it if I do not get relief.

I just remember that each day is another day closer to the next, which can be better. Do I get wound up in my self-pity? Yes, I do sometimes. Some will look down on me for this, but hey, I'm human, am I not?

I have been told that if I really believe, God *will* heal me. I know this can happen, but in my mind, I know God does things for a reason and allows things for a reason. He has allowed this condition to continue for reasons unknown to me. Job did nothing wrong and look at what happened to him; God allowed Job to suffer for a season and Job persevered and endured with his eyes on God.

Look at Paul and the thorn in his side that God allowed. God told Paul that His grace was good enough and that we are made strong in our weakness. So, to those pundits telling me I'm not a good Christian or not faithful enough, I say pick up the Bible and read. Job and Paul persevered and trusted the Lord regardless of what they faced. We can, too.

We all suffer or will suffer in one way or the other, and it is prudent that we learn from those who have suffered before us in order to help us persevere through our own suffering. Through trust and reliance on God, even in the midst of your problems, you can have peace and rest. Sometimes, I feel like I have had enough of this suffering, and I just want to give up.

Give up on what? I do not know. I just want to give up. I get so tired of trials such that even in the midst of my trust, I wish something else would happen. I am not saying I want my life to end or anything like that, but I just want to give up. I want something to change. I want a new chapter in my life. Something refreshing.

In these moments of perpetual misery, the Holy Spirit urges me toward the light of God. Jesus knows what I am going through, and He knows perseverance. He faced both on a level far beyond our comprehension.

In my moments of weakness, when perseverance seems fleeting to my heart, I remind myself that God's strength is with me and refines me through my trials. This helps me to keep going. It helps me to face the day with God on my mind. I can say, yes, He is with me and helps me endure.

I know I must endure, in every facet of my life, spec[ially] those things causing me trouble. It is not just my he[art,] all the other things in life seemingly getting in the way of my walk with Christ.

In Romans 5:3-4, we are told to glory in our tribulations because, when we endure them, they build in us patience and hope—patience in waiting on the Lord and hope in Him as well. When we work to persevere and endure problems in our lives, we desire so much for them to be fixed immediately. We want change that minute and not a second later.

We must have patience in the Lord to help us endure our situations. We need to accept those things we cannot change by ourselves and trust that the Lord is working for our good. Regardless of what we may want in the time we want it, God has His own plans for us. We just need to let go of our wills and let His will be done in us.

For some of us, perseverance is hard to deal with and accept in our Christian faith. We have health, financial, and family problems, just to name a few. We desire quick fixes and quick action from God. When we do not get what we want, we are torn between walking away or drawing nearer to God in that moment. This is the crossroads for us to either hold on to Him or let go.

Keeping faith and hope in God and His grace to help us endure and persevere is paramount in our walk with Him. We do not want to grow stagnant in our relationship with

Him, nor do we want to step away from Him.

What we need and want is His strength. We need to focus on Him the most when we are tempted to throw in the towel. My friends, you just have to persevere. You may need to persevere for a short time, a season, or a lifetime. Regardless, our focus should not be on when or what, but it needs to be on Him. God bless you!

2 Corinthians 4:17: *Our suffering in Christ will not go unrewarded.*

FOUR

BUILDING ENDURANCE FOR THE TRIALS OF LIFE

James 1:2... *"Consider it pure joy, my brothers and sisters, whenever you face trials of many kinds."*

I clearly remember watching TV when I was a young girl growing up in a village called Hlevi in the Volta Region of Ghana. At that time, having access to electricity was very challenging. We usually had to wait until the weekend to watch TV in homes that had generators. From time to time, the programs were interrupted as a result of poor transmission. Then you would hear a loud and annoying noise for thirty or sixty seconds, followed by a prolonged rainbow-color screen. Oh, how I *hated* those disruptions and the *shih!* sounds, because it usually happened at the peak of the programs when we were anxious to know what was to happen next. Since there were no advance warnings of the interruptions in transmissions, there was no way you could avoid it.

The setbacks of life are like that. They often come with no warning, just the announcement: "This is a test." There's often nothing to warn you that the doctor is coming back with a bad report or that a family member is walking out on you. Life's setbacks just show up at the most inopportune times. I had my share of those moments.

We see throughout Scripture that trials are inevitable realities in life, and we read imperatives like this: *"Consider it pure joy, my brothers and sisters, whenever you face trials of many kinds"* (James 1:2). Notice the Bible does not make use of "if you encounter trials," rather it says "when." Trials are inescapable.

Trials are the difficulties we inevitably run into as part of life, not necessarily the problems we create for ourselves. Those problems we create for ourselves are called sins. So, if you are going through a tough time right now, do not be surprised. If you have just exited a trial, do not be shocked when the next one arrives. Trials come with living in an imperfect world.

Trials come in a multitude of colors, shapes, and sizes. So, since we cannot avoid them, what should we do with them? How can we turn a setback into a comeback? The Bible gives us three instructions on how to respond to trials:

1. Recognize the Joy: When trials come, instead of

getting upset and mad, be glad because you know God is up to something good in your life. I can testify to this. *"Consider it pure joy, my brothers and sisters, whenever you face trials of many kinds, because you know that the testing of your faith produces perseverance. Let perseverance finish its work so that you may be mature and complete, not lacking anything"* (James 1:2-4). Yes! Respect the process. This does not mean you have to hide the pain of a trial or pretend the pain feels good. The Bible does not say we need to feel joyful during a trial but to consider that trial all joy.

2. Ask for Wisdom: I like asking questions. God urges us to ask for His help during trials. James goes on to tell us to ask God, and He will freely and generously give us His wisdom (James 1:5). The Bible promises a generous supply of God's wisdom in answer to your prayer, so you will know how to navigate successfully through the trial until you have reached its intended goal.

3. Give God Praise: James' third piece of advice is to give God praise. We are to praise God no matter what our situation (James 1:9-11). Give glory to God. He will lift you to a high position at the right time, and He will humble you when you need humbling. Give Him praise because He knows exactly what you need.

YOU WILL GET THROUGH THIS

God wants you to pass the test—to overcome the trial—not only for Him to give you the reward but also for you to learn to love Him more with Christlike passion and devotion. He walks with you through trials to draw you close to Himself, to teach you to cling to Him, to help you grow spiritually, and to bring you along in your journey towards your comeback. Let Him finish His work in you.

I just want to end with this:

> James 1:12, *"Blessed is the one who perseveres under trial because, having stood the test, that person will receive the crown of life that the Lord has promised to those who love him."*

FIVE

HOW TO HOLD A HURTING HEART

> John 11:33–35..."*When Jesus saw her weeping and saw the other people wailing with her, a deep anger welled up within him, and he was deeply troubled...They told him, 'Lord, come and see.' Then Jesus wept.*"

I do not remember the specific cause of my hurting teenage heart. It may have been an onslaught of teenage drama or a sliver of dim disappointment, a bout with unmet expectations, or a barrage of unkind words. It may have also been due to physical pain from sickle cell crises or seeing that family member who once raped me way back before my tenth birthday, walk into our house the night before pretending nothing had ever happened. But whatever it was, by the time I arrived home from school,

YOU WILL GET THROUGH THIS

I was a hot swirl of ache and tears on that fifteenth day of June 1990.

I yelled at my little brother Nic and sassed my mom. I kicked a basket filled with tomatoes and stomped across the floor. Then, after offending everyone in my wake, I announced I was taking a walk to the riverside. I stormed out the front door without noticing the sullen sky was as angry as I was.

Soon, raindrops tangoed with the tears on my cheeks, and I wished the hurt in my heart would just seep into the puddles at my feet. After a few minutes, I heard the slog of steps on the pavement behind me.

Suddenly, my mom was beside me, her feet keeping cadence with my soggy shuffle. She did not chide me for my outburst or minimize my pain. She did not assure me the sun would shine again or quote Scripture in the rain. On that day, long ago, my mom simply walked with me to the riverside and back home, one soaking step at a time.

In John 11:33–35, we find Jesus sharing steps with a friend in pain, too. Mary's brother, Lazarus, had died, and she was heartbroken and angry. Her prayers had not been answered as she had expected, and her life had been turned upside down.

When Jesus arrived at the scene, He did not diminish her distress or sidestep her sorrow. He just wept with her as they walked to her brother's tomb. What strikes me most about

Jesus' response to Mary's grief is not what He said. *It was what He didn't say.*

Think about it—Jesus knows Mary's weeping will soon turn to joy. He knows that He is going to bring her brother back to life, and all the tears will be trumped by cheers. But Jesus does not use the hope of a better tomorrow to avoid the imminent pain of today. Rather, Jesus holds Mary's heart before He heals it. He enters her pain before He restores her peace.

To be honest, Jesus' example challenges me to consider how I walk with people in my life who may be hurt. Grief can feel uncomfortable and awkward. And far too often, I want to fix someone's struggle instead of sharing in their pain.

Nevertheless, Scripture reminds us that we are not called to resolve someone's tribulation; we are commanded to share the gift of consolation.

> 2 Corinthians 1:3b-4 says, *"...the God of all comfort... consoles us as we endure the pain and hardship of life so that we may draw from His comfort and share it with others in their own struggles."*

We, who have known the compassion of our heavenly Father, are equipped to bring His comfort into any storm.

We do not need to worry about what to say—our imperfect presence often speaks louder than our perfect words. We just need to say "yes" to walking in the rain. Because that is how we walk each other home—one soggy step at a time.

> Romans 12:15... *"Rejoice with those who rejoice, weep with those who weep."*
>
> Matthew 5:4... *"Blessed are those who mourn. They will be comforted."*
>
> Jeremiah 31:13b... *"...for I will turn their mourning into joy. I will comfort My people and replace their sorrow with gladness."*

SIX

SOMETHING HAPPENED IN THAT SMALL CHURCH

John 4:28–29..."Then the woman left her water jar, went into town, and told the people, 'Come, see a man who told me everything I ever did. Could this be the Messiah?"

The second time I heard the name Jesus, I was not that interested. Faith did not make sense to me anymore. I had lost my two beautiful children within a month;

I was forced out of my hometown, so my then-husband could never see me again due to tribal fights.

All the while, I was still serving in the church, but Jesus did nothing to save my children, nor stopped those thirty-one chiefs from convincing my father to bringing up a closure on my marriage.

Life was really hard, and I had already developed a worldview that did not include the name Jesus. In my heart, I was really done with that "Jesus' love stuff."

One day, a gentleman invited me to go to church with him. To be honest, I only went so he would quit asking. It was going to be a one-and-done event.

Something happened in that small church. It was the encounter with Jesus Christ, the Savior of the world. The memory of that encounter still lives with me today. With a heart so tender from hurt it ached, I felt something beautiful that day. It was love, the real kind of love, the kind that snuck past all the wounded places to take up residence. The kind that grew over time to transform my whole life.

In the Bible verse above, we meet another woman who was wounded. She knew about religion, but not a lot about a relationship with God, just like me. She longed to belong and, as a result, had accepted less than she deserved in the pursuit.

Jesus met her at noon at Jacob's well. He was tired and thirsty and asked her for a drink. As their conversation unfolded, we got a glimpse of how Jesus loved so well. By asking a Samaritan woman for water, He made her know she had something to offer. He made space for her honest questions and took time to answer them. He already knew about her broken places and gently led her to a loving heavenly Father. In the end, the Samaritan woman abandoned her water jar and ran to the city. She could not wait to tell others about this encounter. Just like me. I abandoned everything, including my house in Galilea-Kasoa, in Ghana and migrated to America.

> *"Then the woman left her water jar, went into town, and told the people, 'Come, see a man who told me everything I ever did. Could this be the Messiah?'"* (John 4:28–29).

The people in town left what they were doing and made their way to Jesus. He remained with the Samaritans for two days.

> *"And they told the woman, 'We no longer believe because of what you said, since we have heard for ourselves and know that this really is the Savior of the world"* (John 4:42).

What I love most about this is that she did not wait to share her story. There was a good chance some were not going to listen to her. She told them anyway, and it made a powerful impact.

Years ago, when I encountered Jesus in that small church, I also could not wait to share the news. My friends, especially my family, looked at me with doubt. They were not sure what to believe. Some listened, some came to church with me, and some thought I had finally lost it.

Some were changed by His love. When we encounter Jesus, our story can be like a ripple. It drops into the hearts of those who long for the same freedom. Our words may not be eloquent, but that does not mean His miracle is not evident. Like the Samaritan woman, not all will receive our story. Those who do, however, will be drawn a little closer to Jesus. It is He who will speak into their needs, and their encounter will be as personal as ours.

PRAYER

Dear Lord, whether just healed, a work-in-progress, or totally whole, You are doing a miracle in my heart. Help me to continue to share my story and lead that someone closer to You. In Jesus' name, Amen.

SEVEN

SCRUBBING TOILETS FOR THE GLORY OF GOD

> 1 Corinthians 10:31..."*So whether you eat or drink, or whatever you do, do it all for the glory of God.*"

I have the "coolest" job ever! Seriously, every day I get to read the Bible and dive into amazing content to find ways to bless others. Working at BeServed Concierge Services, I get to work with amazing men and women who have dedicated their lives to bringing glory to God through personal touch and the written Word.

Still, there are times I just don't want to go to work. Sometimes, there could be a huge client evaluation looming, and I just can't stand looking at one more spreadsheet while mails are piling up. It is one of those moments I have to use my "gift" of nagging so we can meet client expectations.

It is during those moments of hair-pulling frustrations that I usually reach out to my friend Rebecca Ayettey, aka Aunty Naa (my angel in disguise).

I cannot think of one time when I did not see Rebecca smiling as she diligently went about her work. Cooking for clients in the kitchen was amazingly done by her with a smile. Polishing countertops to shine like nobody's business is also one of the things Rebecca does with a smile.

When there was that huge pile of admin work I had on my desk, while busy trying to make sure clients got their medications refilled on time, Rebecca was always there, helping me clean it with a joyful heart—can you imagine that?

God keeps teaching me through Rebecca that it is not *what we do* but *that we do it for God's glory*. You can be the most consistent Bible reader or a walking theology encyclopedia, but unless you apply God's Word to your daily life, you are empty.

Consider the Pharisees. They were the most biblical literates at the time. They even knew the Law and the message of the prophets from memory, but concerning the state of their hearts and applying Scripture to their lives, they were in the negative zone. Check out Matthew 23 to see how Jesus did not hold back rebuking them:

SCRUBBING TOILETS FOR THE GLORY OF GOD

> *What sorrow awaits you teachers of religious law and you Pharisees. Hypocrites! For you are like whitewashed tombs—beautiful on the outside but filled on the inside with dead people's bones and all sorts of impurity. Outwardly you look like righteous people, but inwardly your hearts are filled with hypocrisy and lawlessness.*
>
> Matthew 23:27–28

When we read God's Word and apply it to our lives, we give God glory and praise. When we live out God's truth, our lives become testimonies of His goodness, and we can bring love and hope to a world that desperately needs it, especially in today's challenging world.

As the key verse says, *"So whether you eat or drink, or whatever you do, do it all for the glory of God"* (1 Corinthians 10:31). In other words, our actions should be inspired and motivated by God's love in order to bring glory to God.

So, whatever I do in this life—whether I am eating or drinking, scrubbing toilets, changing diapers, driving clients to church, cooking for a client, driving clients to doctors' appointments, offering comfort to people after they have lost a loved one, encouraging them to exercise, linking families to the right resourceful agencies, sitting with a client during chemo treatment sessions, grocery shopping for a homebound senior, or finishing one more spreadsheet—I can pray: *How am I honoring God? Lord, may everything I do be for Your glory.*

PRAYER

Dear heavenly Father, thank You for Your amazing Word that helps me grow closer to You. May it never become just something I read but always be a living, breathing, motivating, transforming power in my life. Please forgive me for the times I don't apply it and instead turn to my selfish desires. I pray I never let anything too big or too small stop me from giving You glory. In Jesus' name, Amen.

EIGHT

WHAT IS THE "MORE" GOD WANTS FOR YOU?

> Ephesians 3:20–21…*"God can do anything, you know—far more than you could ever imagine or guess or request in your wildest dreams! He does it not by pushing us around but by working within us, his Spirit deeply and gently within us."*

What are the deepest longings of your heart, that which you desire "more" of in your life yet you're afraid to voice out? You kept it as a secret.

Over the years, I have learned to trust God with the secret desires of my soul. And I can testify to God's faithfulness when it comes to giving me more of His vision, His presence, and His calling, all for a purpose bigger than mine.

Have you ever stopped to wonder what God's response

would be to your heart's cry for "more"? I believe the Savior of the universe would bend down in the most caring of manners and ask, *"More what? And how much more? My supply is unending. My mercy is limitless. My grace is more than you need, and I am all you need!"*

The "more" God wants for your life is beyond comprehension. I love this Bible verse so much: Ephesians 3:20–21, *"God can do anything, you know—far more than you could ever imagine or guess or request in your wildest dreams! He does it not by pushing us around but by working within us, his Spirit deeply and gently within us."*

It changed my thinking and my life when I realized the power of this truth: God can do anything, and not just a little bit more than we dream of, but *far more*.

So, what are your craziest ideas, deepest longings, and grandest plans—the things you have barely allowed your soul to imagine? Even those grand plans are not enough. All of heaven is looking down upon you, shaking its heads, and asking, "Is that all? Is that *all* she wants? Is that all she can dream about?"

Allow me to stretch your thinking because we serve the ultimate Big Thinker, where no plan of yours can ever be compared to His. The amazing truth is, God can take every limitation that has been put on your life—by you or by others—and expand your heart and purpose in a way that will be bigger, higher, and more effective than anything you could imagine. You can never outdream God. But you can absolutely trust Him.

"*Trust in the LORD with all your heart, and do not lean on your own understanding*" (Proverbs 3:5).

"*But, as it is written, 'What no eye has seen, nor ear heard, nor the heart of man imagined, what God has prepared for those who love him'*" (1 Corinthians 2:9).

"*'For my thoughts are not your thoughts, neither are your ways my ways,' declares the LORD*" (Isaiah 55:8).

"*'For I know the plans I have for you,' declares the LORD, 'plans for welfare and not for evil, to give you a future and a hope'*" (Jeremiah 29:11).

"*The heart of man plans his way, but the LORD establishes his steps*" (Proverbs 16:9).

PRAYER

My heavenly Father, I thank You that nothing is ever wasted in our life experiences. The world says, "Just forget about it..." when it comes to our past struggles. But You say, "Just use it! Be fruitful!" Show me ways I can use what I have gone through to help other people. Lord, I pray You will make me fruitful in the land of my suffering. In Jesus' name, Amen.

NINE

HOPE IN THE ONE WHO DOES NOT GROW WEARY

Isaiah 40:31 (NIV)…*"But those who hope in the LORD will renew their strength. They will soar on wings like eagles; they will run and not grow weary, they will walk and not be faint."*

My coffee had been reheated for the third time that morning. A mountain of rumpled laundry mocked me from the couch as I begrudgingly scribbled down my growing to-do list. My princess was playing with her toys in her room, screaming as usual, and I was still wearing my sweaty clothes from an early morning bike exercise.

Had I even brushed my teeth? I honestly cannot answer "yes" or "no" with any certainty. The only things that *were* certain were my souring mood and a wish for the day to be over already.

Why was I feeling so frustrated... *so tired, and burned-out?* Nothing in my life had changed. In fact, my daily stressors were familiar, even expected. The little girl woke up at her normal, crack-of-dawn time. I had a decent sleep and managed to squeeze in a quick workout; the reheated coffee was in my system. I even found a few spare minutes to read through a daily devotion with minimal distractions.

What was I missing? Perhaps more "me" time—more self-care time to better manage myself? A new exercise routine to shake things up and really sweat out my woes? Or stretching? Yes! Maybe try to breathe through those woes instead...or could it be as simple as a pedicure with a friend? Or better yet, a girls' night out? Or maybe I needed more culture. Join a book club? Pick up a new hobby? There had to be something...

As I contemplated how to magically add *extra* hours in the day to complete all the missing self-care tasks, I only became more frustrated. As I let out a long and dramatic sigh of exasperation, a forgotten truth settled heavily over my entire being in that small moment.

These things are all temporary. Sudden clarity and conviction overwhelmed my senses. The feelings I might experience from pursuing any number of self-care remedies were *temporary.*

Did it make any of them bad? Of course not! Taking care

of myself is a good thing; adrenaline rushes are real; freshly scrubbed toes should be appreciated, and nights with good friends are much needed. However, was I to depend on those temporary remedies to wholly sustain my soul through the ups and downs of a chaotic morning, let alone my life? Was it any wonder I was feeling so tired and burned-out?

Suddenly, a word from the Book of Isaiah sprang to the forefront of my mind:

> *Do you not know? Have you not heard? The LORD is the everlasting God, the Creator of the ends of the earth. He will not grow tired or weary, and his understanding no one can fathom. He gives strength to the weary and increases the power of the weak. Even youths grow tired and weary, and young men stumble and fall; but those who hope in the LORD will renew their strength. They will soar on wings like eagles; they will run and not grow weary, they will walk and not be faint.*
>
> Isaiah 40:28–31 (NIV)

Our Lord is eternal. He renews my weary soul with the strength and perseverance I desperately need. *There is no substitute.* My soul exhaled with relief. I did not need to find extra hours in the day for self-care for my sanity. I needed to realign my heart and place my hope in the Lord. It was as simple as that.

Temporary self-care is no substitute for the eternal soul-care only the Lord can provide. And yet, somewhere—amidst the grind of the daily to-dos, the frustrations, and the busyness of life—we lose our way.

Our hearts wander, and we find ourselves clinging to that which cannot sustain us. But we do not have to settle for white-knuckled, clinging hopelessness. We can release our grip temporarily and place our hope in the eternal hands of the One who does not grow weary, the Creator of heaven and earth. He is our Lord. Let us not hesitate to turn our hearts to Him today and every day. His presence in our lives is a promise. It is upon us to claim it.

PRAYER

Dear heavenly Father, I praise You for who You are, the Eternal God. Forgive me for the times I've placed my hope in anything other than You. There is no substitute. I pray You realign my heart to Yours and grant me strength in You alone for this day, in Jesus' name, Amen.

TEN

I FEEL FORGOTTEN

Psalm 43:2..."*For you are God, my only safe haven. Why have you tossed me aside? Why must I wander around in grief, oppressed by my enemies?*"

Thirteen years ago, I was sure God had forgotten me. I had just been released from a detention center. My life was destroyed, and my mind was in a perpetual state of panic. Overall, my life was a mess. For what reason? I had refused to date a married man, someone I called a friend, a former co-worker from Africa. For what? He would come to bail me out, and I would be forced to say yes to his request.

I was drowning in difficult circumstances, confusion, and pain. With each gasping breath, God seemed farther and farther away. I prayed, but God seemed silent. So my emotions began playing tricks on my mind, causing anxieties and fears to get the better part of me.

Instead of feeling God's presence and the strength to trust Him, I felt alone and abandoned in every way. I knew it was not the right way to feel as a Christian, but I felt forgotten by Him nonetheless.

The psalmist in Psalm 43:2 struggled with the same thoughts and emotions as I had…pleading to God, trying to understand why He was letting bad things happen, and why people were hurting him.

It seems the psalmist was at the end of his rope as he expressed his true feelings to God, even asking why it seemed God had tossed him aside. He was questioning God's plans and doubting if He really cared.

Maybe you are experiencing a season of life right now where you feel the same way: tossed aside, rejected, abandoned, disappointed, unwanted, alone, and wondering, like the psalmist, if God has forgotten you.

We all experience these feelings at one time or another, maybe as a little girl or even a woman who desperately wishes her daddy would love her, an employee who longs for the approval of her boss, a woman who would give anything if her husband would pay attention to her, or a husband whose wife has walked away.

Maybe you feel forgotten by friends or family during

the busy holiday season, and loneliness and painful emotions threaten to steal your joy. But although there are countless reasons for us to feel rejected and abandoned in this broken world, feeling forgotten by a Sovereign God can hurt the most.

When we find ourselves feeling this way, we are left with two choices. We can either turn away from God in anger and frustration and develop a sour attitude or allow the words of the psalmist to motivate us to step up in our *faith*, just as he did.

You see, instead of holding on to anger and distrust of God's ways, the psalmist chose to recognize God's sovereignty and sought after Him in the midst of his solitude and confusion. *"For you are God, my only safe haven. Why have you tossed me aside? Why must I wander around in grief, oppressed by my enemies?"* (Psalm 43:2).

We read this in Psalm 43:3: *"Send out your light and your truth; let them guide me. Let them lead me to your holy mountain, to the place where you live"* (NLT). He sought after God, then committed to praise and trust Him no matter what, which is what we read in the next verse, *"There I will go to the altar of God, to God—the source of all my joy. I will praise you with my harp, O God, my God!"* (Psalm 43:4).

Despite his heartache and overwhelming emotions, the psalmist remembered God was truly his only help and that God was always there, never forsaking him even when it felt like it. If you are feeling forgotten by others or by God, raise your hope and let your joy return by intentionally believing that God will never leave you and He is always by your side. Make a commitment to focus on God's presence and the blessings He has given you, and let God be the source of your joy always.

"Can a mother forget her nursing child? Can she feel no love for the child she has borne? But even if that were possible, I would not forget you!" (Isaiah 49:15).

"Long ago the Lord said to Israel: "I have loved you, my people, with an everlasting love. With unfailing love I have drawn you to myself" (Jeremiah 31:3).

A virtuous woman

A courageous, Strong Woman, Dependent solely on God

"Speak up for those who cannot speak for themselves, for the rights of all who are destitute. Speak up and judge fairly; defend the rights of the poor and needy.

The Wife of Noble Character

A wife of noble character who can find?

She is worth far more than rubies. Her husband has full confidence in her and lacks nothing of value. She brings him good, not harm, all the days of her life.

Proverbs 31:8–12 (NIV)

Courage is looking at fear right in the eye and saying,

"Vanish now, I've got things to do."

Faith is seeing light with your heart when all your eyes see is darkness.

ELEVEN

DIFFICULTIES OF LIVING IN A FOREIGN LAND

> Deuteronomy 10:10..."*Now I had stayed on the mountain forty days and forty nights, as I did the first time, and the LORD listened to me at this time also. It was not his will to destroy you.*"

Moving abroad is a major life event for anyone who is brave and blessed enough to take the leap. While being an expat is exciting, fun, and eventful, it can also be challenging. For me, it has been very rough without any family member abroad. I missed especially the hugs from my lovely mom. In fact, I am still going through the process after officially migrating to the US for over eighteen years now.

From making friends to figuring out where to worship,

where to buy groceries, and most importantly, processing of your residency documents without the help of a relation, life as an expat can be very hectic. The difficulties of living in a foreign country can be insurmountable at times.

Behind the lens of social media and the interesting lifestyle projected by folks who live abroad, being an expat can be hard. Here are some of the typical challenges faced by expatriates along with some tips that will make moving abroad a little easier.

Fitting in as an Expat

In life, it is never great to feel out of place. Living in a different culture has a way of making you feel uncomfortable almost all the time. For new expats, it is important to welcome the experience of moving abroad with an open mind.

Knowing that there are more ways of life than the one that you are used to in your homeland will make the journey much easier for you. If you want a label for this mindset, it is called cultural intelligence, and it can be as difficult as mastering or learning a new language.

The biggest thing to keep in mind is the feeling of misfit, which is common, temporary, and can be overcome with a little work. The first ninety days as an expat can be a whirlwind of emotion and frustration, but things will slowly fall in place.

DIFFICULTIES OF LIVING IN A FOREIGN LAND

Make it a point to attend some cultural events in your new country. You can even learn a lot about the culture simply by watching television (probably with subtitles at first). Introduce yourself to your neighbors and invite them for a cup of tea, coffee, or your church's special event if possible or just for simple walk around the block. Ask questions and, in the process, be sure to learn something. These things will all give you some insight into their culture and help ease the feeling of being a misfit.

Making Friends

Getting to know new people in your new country is extremely important. It can be tough for expats to make friends, especially in locations that lack an expat community. However, remaining isolated is not an option and is a surefire way to make your experience miserable.

To meet new people abroad, use every resource possible. This includes searching for meet-up groups online, researching the expat community, especially local churches, and finding expat events online. There are even Facebook groups that cater to the expat community these days. I will encourage you to do your homework right by vetting groups or organizations properly through prayer and interviewing old members prior to any commitment.

The key is to put yourself out there. Like most things in life, the more you put into making friends, the more you will get out of it with good friends. Joining small groups of churches, sports, or volunteering will also expand your social network.

The Language Barrier

While technology can help make language less of a barrier, lack of fluency adds additional challenges to living in a foreign country. When people say to you, "What did you say again?" Or you find them asking "What is she saying?", get to know that you're in trouble with language barrier. However, do not let that stop you from making friends or getting involved in your community events.

Soon-to-be expats should add learning basic phrases to their "moving abroad" checklist. A bit of effort will make a good impression on locals and help you to meet new people. If possible, sign up for language classes—it is not only helpful for linguistic learning but also a great way to meet new people.

Friends from language class will also be just like you—living in a new country where they have a small social circle and do not speak the native language. If they are not available, consider finding online lessons for distance learning.

Distance from Home

It goes without saying that expats can struggle with being far from friends and family. Keeping in touch with loved ones is vital for your mental health and successful stay abroad. The challenge, however, can be finding time to stay connected with them, considering the differences in time zones.

Make it a point to schedule regular conversations with your loved ones and learn the time difference. Luckily, technology can help with this. Setting a regular time for a Skype, WhatsApp, Viber, Facetime video session, or phone call will be helpful for a better life abroad.

Culture Shock

Dealing with culture shock is one of the most common difficulties of living in a foreign country. It happens to most expats, and it creeps in as the excitement of arriving in your new home country fades and reality sinks in. It is hard to understand when it is happening to you, and culture shock affects each person differently.

The experience of moving abroad can be intense and frustrating. You forget how much you earn, and also the everyday tasks you do with ease. In your native country, you just know a lot of things: how to mail a package, what your oven settings are, that is if you are blessed enough to have one at all, you know how to open a bank account, and more. In an expat situation, you are suddenly confused by the easiest tasks, and the frustration can sink in as you navigate the new culture.

Culture shock will inevitably pass. But it is important to monitor your stress level and support the members of your family who are dealing with the same things.

Family and Relationship Strain

Relocating abroad is, of course, made better by having your partner or family with you. However, it can also complicate matters.

Not everyone adjusts the same way or faces the same struggles of moving to a new country. If one person in a relationship follows along and is not working, things get tough. One of you will be experiencing professional highs, while the other may be feeling distraught with a lack of job opportunity and no professional network.

Children can also make things difficult, as they have their own adjustments with new schools and making friends. For them, it can be even tougher because their classmates are less likely to be bilingual than your colleagues and adults you encounter.

It is crucial that you communicate as a family or a couple. Talk to each other and check in, even a daily conversation in the initial months after moving abroad is a good idea. With the help of technology, it is less expensive to communicate with loved ones now than it was for some of us years ago. Make good use of it…stay connected.

You cannot express your feelings too much as an expat, especially because you will have a lot of them. The lows are lower, and the highs are higher, so make sure you have an emotional release. Watch out for signs of expat depression and learn how to manage it if need be. Pray and take care.

TWELVE

GETTING OVERWHELMED WITH LIVING ABROAD

John 16:33 (NIV)..."*I have told you these things, so that in me you may have peace. In this world you will have trouble. But take heart! I have overcome the world.*"

When you first move abroad, so many things might happen at once. You or your partner are usually starting a new job, and you may need to find a place to live. There are all kinds of official documents to sort out and paperwork to file—it gets overwhelming.

It is important to take these "living abroad" challenges one day at a time. Start with the things that will make you most comfortable and know that it is okay if you do not do everything in one week.

Maybe the most important thing to you is to have a normal family meal. After you figure out where to buy groceries, you can learn how to use your appliances. Set up your dining room and kitchen before you take on the rest of the house at your own pace. The rest will happen, and you will feel more in control.

Adjusting to Work in a New Country

Getting used to work seems like a small hurdle, but it is an often-overlooked challenge of moving to a new country. While most people who already live abroad have changed jobs or relocated to a new store or office or factory in the line of their career, it is usually within the same country or even the same town.

Expats have to adjust to working in an unfamiliar culture. The cultural differences and norms in the workplace are as significant as the changes in language, food, and dress around the world. They require respect and some extra work to adapt to the workplace. Make sure you are flexible and open-minded in your new professional and personal life as an expat.

Feeling Unsettled

One of the biggest complaints of expats is the feeling of being unsettled. While some people move abroad because they do not want to be tied down, others live normally after

GETTING OVERWHELMED WITH LIVING ABROAD

some time of being abroad.

Many expats begin their life abroad on a specific contract, and when that contract ends, they need to make another move. When your visa and living situations are tied to temporary employment, it becomes difficult to plan for the future.

If this is the case, the best thing you can do is to firmly decide to make the most of the situation. Creating new ties to your new country makes living life with a little ambiguity bearable. Enjoy the time you have rather than worrying about when it will end.

No matter what, living abroad is an incredible opportunity. While it is not for everyone, it is something you should be proud of and enjoy if you get the opportunity. And remember: these difficulties of living in a foreign country are all easy to overcome, and none of them lasts forever. So, I say, relax and enjoy your new life.

The crucial detail for us to have peace in the middle of everything we face is to stay close to the Lord.

> *"But seek first his kingdom and his righteousness, and all these things will be given to you as well. Therefore, do not worry about tomorrow, for tomorrow will worry about itself. Each day has enough trouble of its own"*
>
> Matthew 6:33–34 (NIV).

THIRTEEN

THE SCRIBBLED TRUTH THAT CHANGED MY LIFE

Acts 3:6 (NIV)...*"Then Peter said, 'Silver or gold I do not have, but what I do have I give you."*

Do you ever struggle with encouraging a friend walking through difficult circumstances? Has someone ever reached out to you with encouragement that deeply impacted your life? Who can you reach out to today? Discover how to help others navigate hard realities with real help from my personal journey.

1 Thessalonians 5:11...*"Therefore encourage one another and build each other up, just as in fact you are doing"* (NIV).

When I lost my baby sister tragically and unexpectedly, my entire world flipped upside down. I was only about eight years old, and they were twins. She died in my arms at the hospital with a beautiful smile on her face. Even though my little brother, her twin survived the storm, it was the first of many very dark seasons of my life.

As years went by, my views began to change about the existence of God. What I once knew to be true suddenly became questionable sometimes. *Is God good? If so, why this? And if I never know why, how can I ever trust God again?* These were tough and honest questions that haunted me, until one day, I got a note from a friend, a girl I affectionately called my "Bible friend." She honestly got on my nerves with all her Bible verses. I was not on good terms with God at that point in my life—I did not even want to believe He existed, and I certainly wasn't reading the Bible.

I made all of this known to my "Bible friend." But in her gentle, sweet, kind way, she kept slipping me notes of truth with verses gently woven in. And one day after returning from a choir practice, one verse cracked the dam of my soul. Truth slipped in and split open my hard-hearted views of life, just enough for God to make Himself known to me.

I held that simple note with one Bible verse scribbled on the front as the tears of honest needs streamed down my cheeks. My stiff knees bent. And a whisper, *"Yes, God,"* changed the course of my life.

My "Bible friend" had reached out to me. And because of her, I am determined to use my words as a gift to others who

THE SCRIBBLED TRUTH THAT CHANGED MY LIFE

may be in hard places, like a friend of mine who recently told me she was struggling with identifying her purpose.

Everything just felt hard, with very little reprieve. If ever there were a drowning with no water involved, this is where my friend is. Maybe you have a hurting friend, too, or know someone who is struggling.

Desperately wanting to love my friend through my words, I sat down to write her a card and sent her a little gift. My heart was full of care, compassion, and a strong desire to encourage, but I struggled to translate all that I felt on paper.

This had been a challenge for me after surviving a mild stroke. As I prayed about it, the word *"loved"* kept coming to mind.

I reminded her she is loved. I reminded her how much I respected her. I reminded her that she is a woman who has so much to offer. I reminded her that she is famous and valuable.

In Acts 3, Peter and John encountered a cripple at the temple gate called Beautiful. They stopped. They noticed. They decided to touch. Riches were not available to them but the ability to value was.

Acts 3:6–7 says, *"Then Peter said, 'Silver and gold have I none; but such as I have give I thee: In the name of Jesus Christ of Nazareth rise up and walk.' And he took him by the right hand, and lifted him up: and immediately his feet and ankle bones received strength."*

Peter and John did not have silver, but they had a hand to offer and value to give. The man in need was worth touching. He was a man who needed someone to see him as a man. He had so much to offer. After he got up, he went into the temple courts, praising and stirring up wonder and amazement about God.

I wanted my friend to remember that she, too, had praise for our God inside her. She can also get up. She can also stir up amazement and wonder about our God.

Yes, she is loved, and God has a good plan for her. I want to help her see that just as my "Bible friend" did for me all those years and continues to do. I will never doubt the power of one woman reaching to the life of another person with some written or spoken whispers of love.

FOURTEEN

FOR OUR OWN AND HEAVEN'S SAKE, WE TELL THE TRUTH

John 14:6 (NKJV)..."*Jesus said to him, 'I am the way, and the truth, and the life. No one comes to the Father except through Me.'*"

John 4:24 (NKJV)..."*God is Spirit, and those who worship Him must worship in spirit and truth.*"

Romans 12:1 (NKJV)..."*I appeal to you therefore, brothers, by the mercies of God, to present your bodies as a living sacrifice, holy and acceptable to God, which is your spiritual worship.*"

YOU WILL GET THROUGH THIS

I must be honest; it has taken me some time to embrace the truth. At times, truth feels so aggressive, ungentle, blunt, and harsh in its reality. Truth did not feel Christian. Rather, it felt unkind.

Being a British-colonized African woman did not help—my culture preferred to sweep truth under the rug and fill the awkward silence with a hot cup of tea or cocoa.

Often, I wanted to live the words of Proverbs 4:23, yet I was sprinting away as if the truth wanted to haunt or hurt me. I created a façade that said my day was fine, that I was not in pain, and I was not scared—whatever I needed to say to belong to the society, to God even, I said it. So long as I was not offending anyone.

I lied to myself, leaving unresolved solutions to my unsatisfactory life. Within the storms we face, all that comes to the surface in the silence, or the chaos, feels antagonistic: the dreams yet to be fulfilled, or perhaps the relationship that is not as paradisiacal as it might appear.

Way before quarantine, distractions could divert our hearts from the truth, especially due to the increased use of social media, but *how helpful were our normal aversions?* Every moment we hid, we missed an opportunity to learn the beauty of God.

The Book of John 4 reminds me of the finest truth-teller that ever lived. Our Lord never avoided honest conversations. He reveled in them. So why would He make space and wait upon the hottest hour of the day for a woman who was already outcast by society? He seeks the honest ones.

Within this dialogue, I discovered a golden nugget that would help me embrace the power of truth forever. The real truth, even if it stung.

I always wondered why Jesus did not tell the Samaritan woman the number of husbands she had but rather asked her to fetch him water to drink. It is because He already knew she had five husbands, and the one she lived with was not her husband.

Jesus was not trying to shame her, nor put her in her place. He is not a rebel of His own teachings; He is a master of them.

Instead, He wanted to see if she would be truthful about her choices. He wanted to see if she was the kind of soil He could sow into, hungry enough for wisdom yet protecting her ego. She didn't tell Him what she thought He'd want to hear. She didn't defend. She simply replied,

> "...I have no husband" (John 4:17b, NKJV).

> "'...in that you spoke truly,' He replied" (John 4:18, NKJV). For true worship, according to our Lord, was coming:

> "God is Spirit, and those who worship Him must worship in spirit and truth" (John 4:24).

Can we ever worship Him if we are not walking in truth? We are missing an opportunity to discover the wonder of His freedom and missing out on life itself.

In the great strength of His undying, never-going-to-leave-you love, we have no excuse to run but every reason to hold on to His hope for us.

For it was there I truly began to grow, where I began to have a change of mentality. I found true stillness in the freedom of *His truth*. I got honest about my fears of abandonment and about my legalism.

I stopped numbing myself to conviction and celebrated the fact that He could trust me with His truth. I finally built trust with myself and my few good friends. The cost of denial outweighed the power of His voice living authentically through me.

Today, I would rather face the sting of my truth than the dull ache of denial, for the distance between myself and God was too brutal to bear.

It was in this divine appointment between the Samaritan woman and Jesus that I learned truth isn't repulsive; it's revelatory. The most freeing worship we could ever know.

"And you shall know the truth, and the truth shall make you free" (John 8:32, NKJV).

FOR OUR OWN AND HEAVEN'S SAKE, WE TELL THE TRUTH

> *Jesus said to her, "Woman, believe me, the hour is coming when neither on this mountain nor in Jerusalem will you worship the Father. You worship what you do not know; we worship what we know, for salvation is from the Jews. But the hour is coming, and is now here, when the true worshipers will worship the Father in spirit and truth, for the Father is seeking such people to worship him. God is spirit, and those who worship him must worship in spirit and truth."*
>
> John 4:21–24

FIFTEEN

WHO DO YOU LISTEN TO?

Psalm 51:6..."*Behold, You desire truth in the innermost being, And in the hidden part You will make me know wisdom.*"

1 Kings 12:8 (NIV)... "*But Rehoboam rejected the advice the elders gave him and consulted the young men who had grown up with him and were serving him.*"

Dear heavenly Father, I know You bring wise people into my life to show me the next step. Give me the maturity and insight to listen to what is wise and what reflects You, for You are my closest counsel. In Jesus' name, Amen.

My head buzzed from the amount of advice I received that day. Social media and advertisements had informed me about what to do, what to think, what to buy, how to parent, and how to win at life. I googled a pressing question, and the options were staggering.

I had just arrived home from a trip with a family member. That person enthusiastically informed me how fast to go, where to turn, and which exit I should have taken.

With all of the massive noise in our ears, it can be very hard to sort through good and bad counsel. It can be difficult and challenging to know how to shut it down when it is unhelpful.

This reminds me of the story of young King Rehoboam of Judah, who was in desperate need of wise counsel. He had been chosen to succeed his father, Solomon.

He met with the people, and they had shared a special request. Though Solomon was considered a great ruler, he had taxed his people heavily and required hard labor.

They asked for a king with a gentler touch. Remember, Rehoboam turned to a group of elders for advice, who told him to give the people what they asked. They said if he did what they advised, the people would follow him gladly.

> *"But Rehoboam rejected the advice the elders gave him and consulted the young men who had grown up with him and were serving him"* (1 Kings 12:8).

WHO DO YOU LISTEN TO?

The next sets of advisors were younger and less experienced. They said Rehoboam should lay a heavier burden on the people and be unmerciful to them.

He took the unwise counsel. He shared the news with the people, who in turn revolted. Nations divided. As a result, Rehoboam became king over just two tribes rather than twelve...all because he listened to (and acted on) unwise counsel.

Like Rehoboam, there can be numerous voices that arise when we need answers – that can produce uncertainty, but we have options.

James 3:17 tells us to seek wisdom, defining it as, *"first of all pure; then peace-loving, considerate, submissive, full of mercy and good fruit, impartial and sincere."*

When we do not know whom to listen to, we can measure it by this biblical standard, asking these questions:

- Does this person stand to gain something if I follow his or her advice? (Impartiality).

- Does this counsel lead to God's best for me or God's best in this situation? (Good fruit).

- Does this person's life reflect the qualities I hope to have in my own life? (Purity, love for peace, consideration, submission or obedience, mercy, and sincerity). If the answer is "no," they do not get to speak into my life.

Second, we examine our own motivation. It is tempting to take unwise counsel because it makes us feel good in the moment, or when it affirms what we want to do, even if it is not the right thing.

But...*is it wise?* That is what directs us, not feelings or seeking an easier route. We can be assured there will always be people telling us what to do or what we should be doing, but thankfully, we are never lost in the noise. We listen, we act on what is wise, and toss out the rest.

> *"I will instruct you and teach you in the way you should go; I will counsel you and watch over you"* (Psalm 32:8).
>
> *"A poor, yet wise lad is better than an old and foolish king who no longer knows how to receive instruction"* (Ecclesiastes 4:13).
>
> *"Do not pay attention to every word people say, or you may hear your servant cursing you—for you know in your heart that many times you yourself have cursed others"* (Ecclesiastes 7:21-22).
>
> *"Listen to my instruction and be wise; do not ignore it. Blessed is the man who listens to*

me, watching daily at my doors, waiting at my doorway. For whoever finds me finds life and receives favor from the Lord" (Proverbs 8:33-35).

SIXTEEN

CHURCH IS MEANT TO BE A GRACE TRIP, NOT A GUILT TRIP

Hebrews 10:25... *"And let us not neglect our meeting together, as some people do, but encourage one another, especially now that the day of his return is drawing near."*

Utterly very exhausted and way too tired to clean up after dinner or get ready for bed… that defined my Saturday night as I conked out on the couch after getting my kiddo to sleep. This was followed by a miserable combination of 2 a.m. insomnia, finally falling back asleep at 3 a.m., only to be startled back awake by my little kiddo and then woken up again by a false alarm on my clock blaring at 6 a.m.

I dozed off, only to wake up right in time to leave for church, with a serious case of the Sunday morning blues. Although I live only about twenty minutes away, every fiber of my being wanted to stay home, snuggled in my comfy PJs. *Please God, don't make me do this. Can't I just skip church today?* I tried to convince myself that it didn't matter if we showed up or not.

Ultimately, I decided to go, even if we were late and by some miracle, we arrived few minutes before the sermon began. And yes, I missed praise and worship. Guess what the topic was! The Prodigal Son. *Oh, isn't that just like the enemy of this world wants me to forget how much God loves me when I feel like running away? Surely, the enemy wants to leave me in a spiritually isolated place.*

During the message, the Holy Spirit reminded me to keep praying for the prodigals in my life—several who used to be very close to the Lord. He also reminded me that just a few days prior, I had gone for a counseling appointment with a dear friend, and we had started talking again for the first time in more than three years.

Wouldn't the enemy of our souls want me to forget that prodigals can still come home, that our God is still in the business of bringing dead things back to life, and He still abounds in grace?

No wonder the enemy worked overtime to keep me out of church that weekend. Thankfully, I felt enveloped in reminders of God's grace instead.

The verse in Hebrews 10:25 is the antidote for days when we had simply rather skipped going to church. It says, *"And let us not neglect our meeting together, as some people do, but encourage one another, especially now that the day of his return is drawing near."* To me, this says, let's keep connecting with one another and encouraging each other—until Christ's return. We are the church! We must stay connected in order to connect others to the gospel. No matter how tired I get, I am always reminded that I am saved to save others, which means I must not shut the door of my connection to the people of my world.

Digging deeper into the preceding verses, we see that through Jesus, God orchestrated a new covenant for His people. Verse 18 explains, *"And when sins have been forgiven, there is no need to offer any more sacrifices."*

For the Hebrew people addressed in this book, this was major news. *No more sacrifices? Christ's death was enough, once and for all?* This reminder was all about God's infinite grace! And I'm fairly certain the world could benefit from us extending more grace to others!

Whether it is the crazy driver who cuts me off in traffic, the friend who lets me down, or even my own heart when I haven't been the kindest toward the people in my home, spiritually isolating myself leads to all kinds of ungracious activities. Why that? *Because we all benefited from walking in grace.*

We live in a new world that tempts us to abandon corporate worship and walk away from our faith.

But Hebrews 10:25 shows us God never designed church or corporate worship to be a *guilt trip*. Instead, church should be a grace trip—a reminder to keep gathering and encouraging and continuing to show His infinite grace to everyone around us.

Whatever excuses we have for not getting there, God has more than enough grace to go around. You can participate in worship and praise services in the comfort of your home. Who cares if you are praising God in your PJs? Giving Him that pure worship from your heart in your two by four apartment is still good enough for God so long as it is done from a clean heart; God accepts it.

SEVENTEEN

THE END OF MY "WHAT IFS"

Philippians 4:6–8... "*...do not be anxious about anything, but in everything by prayer and supplication with* thanksgiving let your requests be made known to God... Finally, brothers, whatever is true, whatever is honorable, whatever is just, whatever is pure, whatever is lovely, whatever is commendable, if there is any excellence, if there is anything worthy of praise, think about these things."

My chest was tight, and I could not breathe. It was a Friday night after church before a busy weekend, and I was excited about everything ahead of me. *Why couldn't I catch a breath?* It felt like my body yelled, "Something is wrong!" and my mind raced to figure out what.

With my arms wrapped around my middle, I sat still

and prayed. Sure enough, digging into the crevices of recent patterns of thinking, I noticed something. A subtle lie had begun to overshadow them all.

What if I fail? What if I'm not enough for this work?

If it had been a conscious thought, I would have fought it and chosen the truth: *God chooses the least qualified, so He gets the glory. I don't have to measure up.* But the lie pulled me into a spiral, and my body revealed the anxiety that set me spinning.

The enemy has ensnared us with these two little words: "What if?" And he sets our imaginations whirling, spinning tales of doom that lurk ahead.

Anxiety says, "What if?" What if I get too close to this person, and she manipulates me like the other friend I trusted? What if my spouse cheats on me? What if my children die tragically? What if my boss decides that I'm expendable?

Certainly, there are healthy levels of anxiety that signal our brains to be afraid of things truly worth being afraid of—like oncoming traffic.

But if you are like me, we keep finding new concerns to worry about, as if by constant stewing we can prepare ourselves for what's to come. But there is a better way because we have a choice. I learned this after finally becoming a mother in 2013.

We can choose to trust God to give us what we need

today, next week, and twenty years from now, even if our worst nightmares come true. God's promises give us hope in every circumstance. In the end, He will resolve every problem we may face here on earth.

Paul wrote to the Philippian church about this truth, and then he gave us guidance for ridding ourselves of anxious thoughts.

For just a moment, let us zero in on one of these replacement thoughts: *"Whatever is true…think about such things."*

What gets me into trouble is worrying about things that might never happen. But truth is the most powerful weapon I have against the enemy, who is *"a liar and the father of lies"* (John 8:44). So, we fight the enemy with whatever is true—meaning, whatever is real!

When we allow our thoughts to spin out of control with worry and fear, either consciously or subconsciously, we try to play the all-knowing role only God can play. We forget it is actually good news; He is in control, and we are not.

Even when our worst fears come true, God remains our unfailing hope. He gave us a way out of our spiraling anxiety. We have a choice to surrender our fears to God.

Now, change is difficult and may come slowly. But because we have been made new creations, we have the Spirit's power to make the choice for truth. Changing our minds is possible! We can pull the "what if" thoughts out of our heads and replace them with what is true. In so doing, we destroy their power over us!

> Romans 12:2... *"Do not be conformed to this world, but be transformed by the renewal of your mind, that by testing you may discern what is the will of God, what is good and acceptable and perfect."*

EIGHTEEN

AN AGENDA THAT WILL NEVER SATISFY

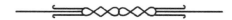

> Mark 3:14-15 (NIV)... *"He appointed twelve that they might be with him and that he might send them out to preach and to have authority to drive out demons."*

I should have been happy. I knew it. I could have listed so many things for which I was thankful for: church activities from week to week, event after event, and year after year most of my life.

So, what was this undercurrent of disappointment that ebbed and flowed just beneath the surface of my honest moments? I got still, and I got sad. Yep! *Very* sad!

I was doing a lot, pouring myself out for God, but not really spending time getting refilled by God. Maybe you can relate, right?

We run at a breakneck pace to try and achieve what God wants us to slow down enough to receive.

He really does have it all worked out. The gaps filled. The needs met. The questions answered. The problems solved. And the parts He has purposed for us. They are all perfectly portioned out in assignments meant for us today. No more. No less.

All He asks is that we personally receive from Him before we set out to work for Him. In doing so, we are fueled by His power and encouraged by His presence. This is the daily sacred exchange where ministry duty turns into pure delight.

How heartbreaking it must be for him when we work like we do not believe He is capable. We say we trust Him but then act like everything depends on us. We give all we have to the tasks at hand with only occasional leftovers of time to slightly acknowledge Him.

Imagine it is like a little girl running while holding a cup, sloshing out all it contains. She thinks what will refill her is just ahead. So, she presses on with sheer determination, clutching an empty cup.

She keeps running toward an agenda God never set, one that will never satisfy. She sees Him and holds out her cup. But she catches only a few drops as she runs by Him because she did not stop long enough for her cup to be filled. Empty cannot be tempered with mere drops. *Oh, poor Little Lucia!*

The tragic truth is what will fill her—what will fill us—is not the accomplishment just ahead. That shiny thing is actually a vacuum that sucks us dry but never has the ability to refill. I should know because that is where I was.

There is no kind of emptiness like when your hands are full, but inside, you are nothing but an exhausted shell. I knew it would take slow moments to get me out of this empty place.

I needed to reconnect with the One who knows how to breathe life back into depleted and dead places. Jesus does not participate in the rat race. He is into the slower rhythms of life like abiding, delighting, and dwelling—all words used to describe us being with Him.

As a matter of fact, when Jesus appointed the disciples, there were two parts to their calling as we see in our key verse, Mark 3:14–15: *"He appointed twelve that they might be with him and that he might send them out to preach and to have authority to drive out demons."*

Yes, they were to go and preach and drive out demons, but the first part of their calling was simply to *"be with him."*

True fulfillment comes when we remember to be with Him before going out to serve Him. He wants our hearts in alignment with Him before our hands set about doing today's assignment for Him.

YOU WILL GET THROUGH THIS

So, He extends what we need and each day, He invites us to receive in prayer, worship, and truth from His Word. And He lovingly replenishes our cup while whispering: *"This isn't a race to test the fastest pace. I just want you to persevere on the path I have marked out especially for you. Fix your eyes, not on a worldly prize but on staying in love with me."*

That is an agenda that is always completely satisfying.

PRAYER

Dear heavenly Father, I'm choosing to stop in the midst of everything to just be with You. My eyes are set on You. Let me never forget what a gift it is to spend this sacred time in Your presence. In Jesus' mighty name, Amen.

NINETEEN

WHEN WE GROW WEARY IN WAITING

Acts 1:4–5 (NIV)..."*On one occasion, while he was eating with them, he gave them this command: 'Do not leave Jerusalem, but wait for the gift my Father promised, which you have heard me speak about. For John baptized with water, but in a few days you will be baptized with the Holy Spirit.'*"

Romans 8:25..."*But if we hope for what we do not see, we eagerly wait for it with perseverance.*"

James 5:7–8..."*Therefore be patient, brethren, until the coming of the Lord. See how the farmer waits for the precious fruit of the earth, waiting patiently for it until it receives the early and latter rain. You also be patient. Establish your hearts,*

YOU WILL GET THROUGH THIS

for the coming of the Lord is at hand."

Are you in a season of waiting on God to move? Do you find yourself tempted to push forward with your plans instead of trusting God's timing? Got Scriptures that encourage you to wait on God's perfect plan? How do you interact with people during your waiting period?

With every step, a piercing pain shot from my heel to the base of my neck. For almost four years, nerve pain had been an unwelcome menace, intruding at the most inconvenient of times. This was an injury from a car accident on February 10, 2017. I was rear-ended by a dump truck filled with garbage in Reston, Virginia, on my way from work.

We were running late for a play, and I still needed to grab the camera, pack the snack bag, and fasten the shoes. I was determined to arrive on time, walking into the science lab as a "picture-perfect family" held together by supermom glue.

In bed that night, with the aid of my two best friends—the heating pad and diclofenac sodium topical gel muscle cream—my princess inquired, "What happened tonight?"

To avoid her gaze, I remained silent, although I knew exactly what had happened. I had ignored my doctor's instructions to rest and wait a few weeks longer before engaging in physical activity. But I told myself, *"You don't need more downtime; you're ready and able to get back into full swing now."*

Enduring physical and spiritual pain, I wrestled with God: *"Why haven't You healed me? Why are You letting my little girl see such a weak momma? She needs me to be strong! I'm not asking to run a marathon; I just want to be able to move throughout the day!"*

Angry that the Lord was "holding me back," I switched off the light, pulled the sheets over my head, and tried to sleep.

Unable to fall asleep, I got up and shuffled into the living room. My mind wandered to a passage I had read earlier during the week: *"On one occasion, while he was eating with them, he gave them this command: 'Do not leave Jerusalem, but wait for the gift my Father promised, which you have heard me speak about. For John baptized with water, but in a few days you will be baptized with the Holy Spirit'"* (Acts 1:4–5).

Jesus spent forty days after His resurrection preparing His disciples to spread the good news. I pictured them eager and excited to begin their mission, yet Jesus told them to wait. They were not to go anywhere until they received the Holy Spirit to go with them.

But the next verse reveals their focus was elsewhere; they wanted to know when Jesus would return to establish the Kingdom of God on earth. Jesus told them they should not worry about that time but rather wait for the Holy Spirit, whom they would need as a witness of all they had seen and heard (Acts 1:7-8).

I'm quick to judge the disciples' response to Jesus' commands, yet I am equally guilty of ignoring God's instructions for today, preferring to focus on my plans for tomorrow.

Jesus knew the disciples would fail in their own strength and the same holds true for us. God wants us to trust Him and attend to His timing even when we think we are ready for action. The tendency to thwart God's timing when life feels like it is moving just a little too slowly was not unique to my situation. Like a queen bee, I often buzz around at my own pace, only to suffer both physical and spiritual consequences. Then, nothing dulls the ache in my sin-stung heart besides confessing my rebellion and surrendering to the Lord's will instead of my own.

In this very present moment, God gives His children the same Holy Spirit for guidance, comfort, and strength that He gave the disciples over two thousand years ago.

When we believe our ways and timing are better than God's, we miss out on the precious gift of full and abundant life lived through the power of the Holy Spirit. Embrace patience and wait on the Lord until He is ready to use you and send you forth.

PRAYER

Dear heavenly Father, thank You for being our strength when we are weak. Please help us to wait on Your perfectly timed plans, fully surrendering our lives to Your leading.

In Jesus' name, Amen.

Five Psalms to Pray When You Feel Overwhelmed

It only takes one look at the world around us to see that we are living in an overwhelming time in history. *We are overwhelmed with COVID-19 pandemic, racism, oppression, politics, heartache, technology, social media, information, education, conflict, relationship struggles, and we are even overwhelmed with life.* But God's Word offers the help and hope we need in these challenging times.

Our best go-to resource is the Word of God. *No substitute*!

Sometimes when we are overwhelmed, we turn to friends for help, or to family for support. But the one place we will find true help and support is at the feet of Jesus. So, let us go there. Let us bow at His feet and pray these Psalms in these overwhelming days:

(1) Psalm 56

Feeling overwhelmed and need God's protection?

Take time to read through the entire Psalm and you will quickly see that this is a *prayer* to pray in moments of fear and attack. When we need God's protection, sometimes we try to suit up with our own strength. But we cannot fight our battles and expect to win without God's protection and strength. It requires us to trust God and believe His Word even when we feel surrounded. My favorite verses I prayed from this Psalm were Psalm 56:3 and Psalm 56:11. *"When I am afraid, I put my trust in you"* (Psalm 56:3). *"In God I trust; I shall not be afraid. What can man do to me?"* (Psalm 56:11).

(2) Psalm 57

Feeling overwhelmed and need God's mercy?

Sometimes I cry out for God to have mercy on other people, but when my own heart needs mercy, it is hard to admit. Although I want to receive God's mercy, it requires that I admit I have a need. When I'm brought to my knees by overwhelming circumstances, I'm positioned to receive God's mercy.

Maybe you can relate. You want God's mercy, but it is hard to receive unless you feel a deep need in your soul.

The verses in this chapter to lift as a prayer when you are overwhelmed is Psalm 57:4–5. Pray these verses out loud and print them out.

"My soul is in the midst of lions; I lie down amid fiery beasts— the children of man, whose teeth are spears and arrows, whose tongues are sharp swords. Be exalted, O God, above the heavens! Let your glory be over all the earth!" (Psalm 57:4–5).

(3) Psalm 58

Feeling overwhelmed and need God's justice?

There has never been a time in my life that I have felt the need for justice more than now. Maybe you feel it too. Your heart might feel overwhelmed and not even know what to pray. But the psalmist expresses the heart's cry of one who longs for justice. It might feel odd to pray such a declarative portion of Scripture, but I am reminded through these verses about the truth that God's righteousness always wins. God is a righteous judge and He does not approve of injustice. *"The righteous will rejoice when he sees the vengeance; he will bathe his feet in the blood of the wicked. Mankind will say, "Surely there is a reward for the righteous; surely there is a God who judges on earth"* (Psalm 58:10–11).

(4) Psalm 59

Feeling overwhelmed and need God's defense?

When my heart feels offended, I sometimes feel the need to defend myself. But this Psalm reminds us that God is our defender. We do not always need to have the last word or share every thought that goes through our heads. Often, the best thing we can do is simply tell God all about it.

I love this Psalm when I feel overwhelmed because it expresses the cry of my heart in the beginning and ends with praise to the Lord. It is a strong reminder that sometimes, the hard things that consume my heart and mind are the very things that lead me to the feet of Jesus. *"But I will sing of your strength; I will sing aloud of your steadfast love in the morning. For you have been to me a fortress and a refuge in the day of my distress. O my Strength, I will sing praises to you, for you, O God, are my fortress, the God who shows me steadfast love"* (Psalm 59:16–17).

(5) Psalm 60

Feeling overwhelmed and need God's help?

Help! When life gets full and my heart cannot speak, this is the only word that I can manage to utter in prayer. But Psalm 60 fills in the blanks for me when my words are lacking. Sometimes, we think if we pray just right, God will answer. But when we turn to God with a sincere heart, the words are not so much the key as is the heart. And I am so thankful God is my help. *"Oh, grant us help against the foe, for vain is the salvation of man! With God we shall do valiantly; it is he who will tread down our foes"* (Psalm 60:11–12).

Do not worry; God is taking care of you. Even if it may seem you are all alone.

Remember that each one of us is a child of God, and he takes care of us at each and every moment. You might feel aloof and lonely, but that does not mean that God isn't by your side. He is always there to help you out against all odds.

It is none other than the Almighty who knows the ins and outs of everything that you have been going through! God takes care of each one of us. It might seem as if you do not have anyone in your surroundings, and you are fighting all alone in the battle of your life, but trust me, there is nothing as such.

We all have to fight our own battles, and God puts us in those wars only to test if we are potent enough to combat the situation. God takes care of each one of us, so there is nothing to worry about!

You might seem to be all alone, but make sure that you are not losing your hope. There's nothing to lose your hope upon, for God is always there to help you out from all hardships.

YOU WILL GET THROUGH THIS

When you feel that you have lost all ways, and there's nothing that you can do, that's when miracles take place. The Almighty puts you in several tests just to check out if you are good enough to retain your position despite all the hurdles.

However, all that He wants to see is whether or not you are actually putting your efforts into it. A lot of us simply ignore the situation and let things go, wondering as if nothing would do good.

On the contrary, there are a couple of people who believe in themselves and the path of God. They are the ones who put effort into thinking that it is only the efforts that make miracles happen.

Remember that God stays by the latter's side. He stays beside you and helps you in every possible way, thereby making sure that you always have the upper hand to guide yourself.

Remember that in life, each one of us has got his/her own clock. There is absolutely no point to gear yourself up just by seeing others. If someone has achieved something, that does not necessarily mean that you will have to achieve that particular thing in your life.

It is essential to understand that things are meant to happen as per their own timings, and nothing will occur as we want them to turn up.

At times, you may be on time, while at other times,

you will probably be a little late in doing the same thing. However, that happens, and these are just parts and pieces of our lives.

You may, at times, take a little longer than the others, and you might be slow at certain things. While others have already completed a task, you might be the one who is lagging behind.

However, make sure that you are not allowing yourself to feel low and heartbroken about that! You should have the potential to understand and accept things as they are and keep going!

Remember that at the end of the day, nothing can count more than your own efforts. You need to try your maximum, and even if things do not fall in place, it is totally fine. That is none of your mistakes, and you will have to accept it as a part of the process.

You must know that life is all about learning, even if things did not turn in your favor. All that should matter to you are the lessons that you have learned in the process.

It is important to remember that we never fail while trying. In each and every trial, we just keep on learning and eliminating the odds.

However, it is important to understand that life will show you different chapters and each one of them will look different in its own unique way. At times, you need to move with the flow and accept the fact that you cannot control each and every thing.

It is important to understand that life will keep on going, and you will have your own time to work and be successful as well. Just follow as things are meant to be, and everything will automatically fall in its place.

God is taking care of you, even when it seems like you're all alone; believe me, God is working hard behind the scenes of your life.

CONCLUSION

Finding our purpose and God's direction in our lives are two of the continual challenges we face as Christians. However, I believe with prayer, discernment and strong faith in His Word, it is possible to live a victorious life every day. *Keep living! Keep winning!* You will get through this.

NOTES

YOU WILL GET THROUGH THIS

YOU WILL GET THROUGH THIS

YOU WILL GET THROUGH THIS

YOU WILL GET THROUGH THIS

CPSIA information can be obtained
at www.ICGtesting.com
Printed in the USA
BVHW050449061121
620874BV00007B/108